FROM SUGAR TO SNEAKERS TO SIMPLE

FROM SUGAR TO SNEAKERS TO SIMPLE

LESSONS LEARNED ON ONE WOMAN'S JOURNEY TOWARDS HEALTH AND A BALANCED LIFE

Helen Granskog

Published by: Simple Press, Essex Junction, Vermont
Editing by: Dr. Louise Edje
ISBN: 1540491153
10 9 8 7 6 5 4 3 2 1

Dedicated to my amazing mother,
whose example and love helped me
become all that I am.

Foreword

Helen and her friend, Rosa, were helping a small group of us prepare for the Hebron Fuel Run. At 250lbs I decided to run/walk my first 5k. This was my first real opportunity to get to know Helen. As Helen and Rosa trained and prepared those of us who were participating in the race, I spent time walking and talking with Helen. A friendship was built that would encourage us through the many changing seasons of both of our lives. Amazingly years later, after changes to my life and career, our roles reversed as Helen sought me out, as a coach and personal trainer, to improve her speed and performance in her Half Ironman Triathlon.

Most of my adult life I have been overweight, obese, or worried about being overweight or obese. At the time I ran my first 5k I was extremely out of shape, and it took everything I had to walk the distance. I had yo-yo dieted most of my teenage and adult life. I feel that Helen's journey can resonate with the part of us that strives for that perfection, and falls short, or might feel lost in a sea of hopelessness or even at times apathy. I experienced each of these emotions at different times when my life was out of balance. Striving for balance is not about finding perfection in each area, but about making manageable changes or baby steps as we move towards what is balance for each one of us. No one can say what true balance is for another person. We each have to search within ourselves to find what is best for us to bring happiness, health, wellness, spirituality and balance in life. I believe Helen's book delves into the different areas in our daily journey in life, and helps us consider each aspect as we do some self-reflection. This is a book that could be used and enjoyed over and over again as we move through our life. As we grow, our families and lives change as we age. The one thing that is always necessary is to find balance in our ever-changing life.

Liz Krams
Certified National Academy of Sports Medicine
Personal Trainer

Acknowledgements

I am forever indebted and grateful to my mother, Dr. Louise Edje, for being an amazing example of health and balance throughout my life. In the midst of a busy life I appreciate her taking time to be my editor. I am grateful for my siblings Marietsa McCreary, Dr. Louito Edje and Otoma Edje who have played a big role in supporting my life adventures and contributed their insights and comments to this story.

This work would not have been possible without Rosa Fontanez whose relationship and vision started me on this journey towards health and balance 17 years ago. I am grateful for my coach, Liz Krams, who has stood by my side throughout the years and continues to help me reach my goals. Kristen Balzer's contribution on format and design was invaluable. I appreciate my many friends who have stood by me and supported me through the transformation to health and balance.

Nobody has been more important to me in the pursuit of this project than the members of my family. I would like to thank my loving and supportive husband, Dr. Karl Granskog, who always encouraged me to follow my dreams. I am grateful for my two wonderful daughters, Evelyn and Alexandra, who provide constant encouragement and energy.

"Let us not become weary in doing good, for at the proper time we will reap a harvest if we do not give up."

Galatians 6:9

Table of Contents

Introduction

I am a 42-year-old woman with a husband and two daughters. Evelyn is 8 years old and Alexandra is 7 months old. I love to run, bike and swim. I have completed 2 marathons and 2 half Ironman races. On the way to reaching these goals I completed many triathlons and road races, as many as 13 races in one year.

My diet consists of food that is organic and homemade. I make my own personal care items and household cleaning supplies using all natural ingredients. "Helen's Simple", my personal care business, and "Your Balance", my coaching practice, are being established at the time of this writing. My life wasn't always like this, I have not always been health-conscious and interested in being the best that I could be physically, emotionally and spiritually.

I grew up in Malawi, Central Africa in a household with both parents and three siblings. We all enjoyed family meals, a fresh vegetable garden, home-cooked meals, great morning and evening routines, a sense of community, family vacations, active free time and supportive parents.

An amazing foundation was laid throughout my childhood. During high school my family moved to America where things changed for me. Despite the experiences of my childhood, I did not let them have a lasting impact on the way I lived as an adult. When I moved out of my parent's house, I chose to eat mainly processed foods, neglect my sleep, drink a lot of soda, eat a lot of sugar, I did not take time for my own needs and I did not exercise consistently. As a result of my choices, my health and wellbeing suffered.

This book will take you through my 17-year journey towards health and balance. I will share the information and lessons I learned along the way that helped to inform my decisions. The book is broken into 3 sections that best capture the different phases of my life over the 17 years From Sugar to Sneakers to Simple. Within each chapter, I will take a deeper dive into my life as it relates to the topic, look at the impact of my choices, the information I discovered and the lessons I learned. At the end of each chapter there is an assessment statement for you to consider and three questions to help you reflect on your own life as it relates to each topic discussed.

Part One

I WANT
SUGAR

1

Sugar

During my childhood in Malawi, Central Africa, my family had a vegetable garden that allowed us to have fresh vegetables on a daily basis. My family ate balanced meals and we only had sweets as part of a special occasion. As a child I had a sweet tooth but it was controlled and I did not over-indulge. As I became an adult and lived on my own my diet was abysmal because I chose to eat lots of fast, processed food.

A regular part of my diet was a candy bar and a can of soda every day at lunch. I had copious amounts of soda as I enjoyed the taste and carbonation. I had a deathly addictive sweet tooth when it came to sugar, I exercised very little control over how much chocolate I ate. The candy jar at home was a bottomless pit and forever full. I also chose to drink a lot of tea. Growing up it was customary for us to have tea every day at 4 o'clock, which became part of my daily habit as an adult and I grew to love a large cup of tea with lots of sugar and cream. My irresistible sugar craving was never satisfied; I always came back for more and continued to add more and more sugar to my tea. As I look back now, I see and understand how addictive and damaging all the processed food and added sugar was to my health.

Refined sugar can be considered a poison as it has been stripped of all its vitamins and minerals. What is left is nothing but refined carbohydrates that the body cannot use in its present state. Without the missing elements, the carbohydrates we ingest are not metabolized properly and can lead to a host of physiological problems. Sugar also drains the body of vital minerals and vitamins due to the demand required for digestion, detoxification and elimination. If sugar is part of a daily diet, it produces an acidic state and more and more minerals are needed by the body to restore the imbalance created. The constant drain on the system will eventually affect every organ of the body. As a result, you can experience fat storage, an abnormal blood pressure, poor circulation, poor brain function and suppressed immune function.[1]

Dr. Weston A. Price, a research dentist, concluded that as soon as refined, sugared foods were imported into a "primitive" diet as a result of contact with "civilization," physical degeneration began in a way that was definitely observable within a single generation. Sugar's only contribution to one's diet is caloric energy and a habit-forming taste, nothing else. The rest of the foods we consume contain some nutrients in the way of proteins, carbohydrates, vitamins or minerals, or all of these.[1]

Many of the foods we eat are converted into glucose in our bodies. Glucose is always present in our bloodstream, and it is often called "blood sugar". Dextrose, also called "corn sugar," is derived synthetically from starch. Fructose is fruit sugar. Maltose is malt sugar. Lactose is milk sugar. Sucrose is refined sugar made from sugar cane and sugar beet. Glucose has always been an essential element in the human bloodstream. Sucrose addiction is something new in the history of the human animal.[1]

Any eating plan that does not take into account the quality of carbohydrates and make the distinction between natural, unrefined carbohydrates such as whole grains and vegetables and man-refined carbohydrates like sugar and white flour is dangerous. The foundation of a sensible eating lifestyle should include eliminating sugar and white flour and replacing them with vegetables and natural fruits that are in season. The quality of your health and life can be radically improved by changing the quality of carbohydrates you eat.[1]

Lessons Learned

Natural sugars found in fruits are okay for me to consume but I have to limit chocolate and added sugar because of its addictive and negative effects on my body. I have regularly chosen to go without sugar in my diet altogether for large periods of time.

Step back and consider...
...how prevalent sugar is in society.

Have you thought about.....

1. ...how much sugar you consume daily?
2. ...the impact sugar is having on your body?
3. ...how you can reduce the sugar in your diet?

2

Water

Growing up, water was the primary beverage in my household. We only had soft drinks as part of a special occasion, when we went out shopping or had guests over. I enjoyed drinking water and drank it often. As I became an adult, I chose to drink a lot of soda and tea with cream and sugar. I rarely drank water. I drank so much soda that I lost my taste for water and did not drink it saying it did not taste good. I had a soda daily during lunch, a large cup of sweetened tea was my preferred beverage whether home or away. I drank so many carbonated beverages and so much tea that my husband was concerned about my fluid intake. At the time I did not understand his concern, I do now, as our bodies are 75% water. This is a very important fact to know, as we consider the beverages that we drink and their effects on our body.

We often get thirsty and grab a drink of any liquid thinking it will satisfy our thirst and give our body what it needs. Any liquid of choice will not quench our thirst nor will it give our body what it needs over the long term. The liquids other than water we reach for may often act as a diuretic and dehydrate us instead of hydrate us. Since our body consists of so much water it is imperative that we give it water not just any liquid. The functioning of our cells and organs depends on our regular intake of water. Drinking water should take place throughout the day, not just when we feel thirsty. Thirst is the last sign of dehydration, not the first as is commonly thought. When we do not replenish the water that our bodies loose through a variety of daily activities like breathing, exercising and going to the bathroom, we can damage our cells and organs in an irreversible way.[2]

If we do not properly hydrate our bodies with water, we run the risk of having a whole host of different conditions; dry skin, dark colored urine, fatigue, allergies, early signs of aging and asthma to more serious conditions like high blood pressure and heart disease. Some often overlooked symptoms of chronic dehydration are heartburn, constipation, urinary tract infections, autoimmune diseases such as chronic fatigue syndrome and multiple sclerosis, high cholesterol and weight gain. You should drink enough water to turn your urine light yellow, if it is not increase your intake. If you are outside on a hot day or engaging in strenuous activity, it is very important that you increase the amount of water you drink. As you age, your thirst mechanism works less efficiently so older adults need to pay more attention to the color of their urine to see if their water intake is adequate. Drinking an adequate amount of water daily will help you maintain a healthy body weight, properly digest food, absorb nutrients from food, have healthy, glowing skin, decrease muscle and joint inflammation, have better circulation and detoxify your body naturally.[2]

When it comes to water, there's more to choose from than simply tap versus bottled. Plain tap water is easy, convenient and it comes right out of your kitchen faucet. However, most tap water is contaminated with a lot of pollutants that increase your risk of serious health problems. Some of these contaminants are arsenic, aluminum, fluoride, prescription and over-the-counter (OTC) drugs and disinfection byproducts (DBPs).[3]

Each of these contaminants affects us in a different way. Arsenic is a powerful carcinogen; aluminum increases your risk of Alzheimer's, Parkinson's and liver disease; fluoride can weaken the immune system and accelerate aging, prescription and OTC drugs can lead to birth defects and DBPs, substances that form when water is disinfected, are also cancer promoting. Sadly bottled water may not be any better as 40 percent of it is said to be tap water. Other options for water include; distilled water, ionized water and vitamin water. All of which have health concerns associated with them.[3]

The most cost effective and environmentally sound choice you can make is to buy and install a home water filtration system. There are three different types of water filters to consider; reverse osmosis filter, ion exchange filter, and granular carbon and carbon block filters. A reverse osmosis filter will remove about 80 percent of the fluoride and most disinfection byproducts but the drawback is the cost and need to have a plumber install it. The ion exchange filter is designed to remove salts in the water, like calcium. Granular carbon and carbon block filters are the most common counter top and under the counter filters. Granular activated carbon is recognized by the EPA as the best available technology for removing organic chemicals like herbicides, pesticides and industrial chemicals. Carbon block filters offer the same great filtering ability but are compressed with the carbon medium in a solid form. By combining different media, you can remove a wide range of contaminants. As you consider which system is best for you, select a filtration system that offers a variety of methods to remove many different contaminants, also consider the pH balance. The ideal pH of your water should be between 6.5 and 7.5, which is neutral.[3]

Lessons Learned

Plain, clean water is necessary and vital frequently throughout the day in order for me to be in optimal health and for my body to function properly. It is critical for detoxification and cell function. When I was not giving my body the water it needed I suffered from migraines, poor circulation and dry skin.

> *Step back and consider...*
>   ...when you drank your last glass of water.

Have you thought about.....

1. ...how much water you drink every day?
2. ...how clean is the water you drink?
3. ...how you can provide the cleanest water for yourself and your family?

3

Processed Food

My mother has always been an amazing cook. As a child my siblings and I enjoyed eating fresh fruits and vegetables and homemade dishes from many different countries. Since my father was a professor of agriculture, I grew up on a college campus where my neighbours came from a wide variety of places such as Nigeria, Philippines, India and England. We participated in Sundowners every week. This was a time when we met with our neighbors and enjoyed a potluck dinner together. The adults talked and the children played. The Sundowners gave me a varied palate and exposed me to great cooking as my mother learned how to cook many of the dishes prepared by our neighbors.

Aside from introducing me to a variety of foods through her cooking, my mother was a great vegetable gardener. I remember rows of different vegetables such as tomatoes, carrots and peas growing in the back yard and fresh herbs such as mint and parsley growing in a barrel. We always had vegetables as a snack and part of our meals. Sadly when I left home as a young adult after moving to America I did not maintain the healthy lifestyle I was exposed to as a child. I moved away from the fresh homemade foods and gravitated towards processed, packaged foods. I chose to eat fast food and microwavable meals. My meals consisted of things like bacon double cheese burgers, buttered toast, packaged beans and rice, microwave sausages and jarred spaghetti sauces, I rarely took time to prepare a meal from scratch as my mother had. Fruits and vegetables were no longer a staple part of my diet. As a result of my processed food choices my health and wellbeing suffered.

To enjoy optimal health, 90 percent, or most, of your allotted food budget should be spent on whole foods and only 10 percent should be spent on processed or packaged foods. Whole foods are fresh fruits, vegetables, nuts, seeds and beans.[4] The closer most of the food you eat is to nature, the better. The term "processed food" refers to foods that are chemically processed, made from heavily refined ingredients and artificial additives.

There are many reasons why processed foods are not healthy:

1) Processed foods are high in sugar and/or high fructose corn syrup. Excess sugar consumption is linked to a host of conditions such as insulin resistance, high triglycerides, heart disease, diabetes, obesity, and cancer. Refined fructose, typically in some form of corn syrup, is now found in just about every processed food you can think of, and fructose actually "programs" your body to consume more calories and store fat. Fructose is primarily metabolized by your liver,

which is the only organ that has the transporter for it. High amounts of fructose tax and damage your liver in the same way alcohol and other toxins do. Fructose, just like alcohol, is metabolized directly into fat and gets stored in your fat cells. Once fructose is stored in your fat cells it can lead to mitochondrial malfunction, obesity, and obesity-related diseases, especially if you are insulin or leptin resistant. Leptin resistance is when the brain does not register that you have had enough to eat and are full.[5] The more fructose or high fructose corn syrup is consumed in food, the worse it is for overall health. It is a good idea to limit daily fructose intake from fruit to 15 grams or less. Additional fructose will be consumed from beverages other than water and processed food.

2) Processed foods are manufactured to cause overeating. Our bodies are designed to naturally regulate how much food we eat and the amount of energy we burn. Food manufacturers know how to over-ride our biological regulators and design processed foods that are engineered to be "hyper-rewarding" and very easy to overeat.

3) Processed foods contain many artificial ingredients. Processed foods may contain dozens of artificial chemicals such as preservatives, artificial colors, artificial flavors and texturants. Despite the fact that food manufacturers often claim that artificial food additives are safe, research says otherwise. Preservatives have been linked to health problems such as cancer and allergic reactions. Nine of the food dyes that are currently approved for use in the US are linked to health issues ranging from cancer and hyperactivity to allergic reactions. Artificial flavoring has several concerning properties for brain health and may trigger Alzheimer's disease.

4) Processed foods are addictive. Processing modifies or removes important components of food, such as fiber, water, trace minerals and nutrients, changing the way they are digested and absorbed by your body. Whole foods contain a mixture of carbohydrates, fats, proteins, fiber, and water to help you feel satisfied, while processed foods stimulate dopamine, a feel-good neurotransmitter, making you feel good even though you are missing necessary nutrients and fiber. Artificial dopamine stimulation can lead to excessive food cravings and food addiction.

5) Processed foods are high in refined carbohydrates. Refined carbohydrates like breakfast cereals, bagels, waffles, pretzels, and most other processed foods quickly break down to sugar in the body bringing with it a host of problems. Processed foods are low in fiber—unless you regularly eat whole fruits and vegetables, nuts, and seeds, you are missing out on healthy forms of fiber. Prepared foods that are made with large amounts of trans fats and processed vegetable oils promote inflammation, which leads to most chronic and serious diseases. Due to their chemical instability, consuming oxidized vegetable oils has been linked to health problems, such as atherosclerosis and heart disease.[6]

The solution to improving your health and losing weight can be as simple as crowding out processed foods with real, organic whole food. People have thrived on vegetables, meats, eggs, fruits, healthy fats and other whole foods for centuries. I believe most people need between 50 and 70 percent of their daily calories in the form of healthy fats. Olives, olive oil, coconuts, coconut oil, organic butter, organic raw nuts, organic pastured eggs, organic cheeses, pastured meats and avocados should be included in your meal planning.[6] Visit your local farmer's markets for in-season produce and plan your meals accordingly. Eliminating processed foods from your day requires that you take time weekly to plan your meals and snacks in advance. You can generally plan a week of meals to make sure you have on hand all the necessary ingredients. Once meals have been planned do any prep work ahead of time so that dinner is easy to prepare if you are short on time in the evenings. Lunch the next day can be leftovers from the previous night. Eliminating processed foods can retrain your body to burn fat instead of sugar, a key component of health and weight loss.

Lessons Learned

Processed foods are engineered to taste good and be irresistible but have little nutritional value. They are made with preservatives, additives and ingredients that do more harm than good to my body when I eat them. The time spent cooking from scratch and eating whole foods and healthy fats is always worth it.

Step back and consider...
...the food sitting on your kitchen shelves and in the refrigerator.

Have you thought about.....

1. ...how much of what you eat is processed?
2. ...how the processed foods you eat are impacting your health?
3. ...which of your favorite meals can be made at home?

4

Lifestyle

My lifestyle was very busy and hectic. As a newly married couple we did not have children yet so I threw myself into my social life. I enjoyed being around people and was rarely home. My husband and I led the youth group in our church and I was always with the teens after work. It was very important to me that I help the teens draw near to God but in the process my life was thrown out of balance. In my desire to serve I was out most nights of the week spending little time with my husband. In the morning we would communicate in passing about the details of the home and schedule of the day and not see each other until later that evening only to do it again the next day. I was not taking time for my husband and myself.

Life is not supposed to be like this. We are not supposed to be rushing around with a hectic schedule taking care of everyone but ourselves and those most dear. As we race through meals, work, family time and social events we miss many pleasures that we are in too much of a hurry to notice or appreciate. [7] A balanced lifestyle involves taking time for all aspects of life such as relationships, work, fitness, health and emotional wellbeing. It is also very important to engage in stress relieving activities on a regular basis. Some stress relieving activities can be a time to just sit and relax, savoring a cup of tea, finding a hobby, going for a walk and enjoying a good laugh with a friend.

To further help reduce stress find an exercise you enjoy and can do regularly.[8] I enjoy running regularly but the exercise you engage in can be walking, playing volley ball, hiking or biking. Even a few minutes of exercise can have amazing physiological effects and elevate your mood. It is important to spend time with family building connections, talking and sharing experiences together. Family relationships are foundational and need to be given special time and attention whether you have children or not. Taking time to cook and eat a nutritious meal at home with your family is critical to living a balanced lifestyle that leads to wellbeing. A healthy meal will boost your mood and give you the energy you need throughout the day. A chosen career or job can have a significant impact on your wellbeing. It is important to enjoy the work you do and create an environment that feeds you and not drains you emotionally. If the work you do is emotionally draining and challenging, it is imperative that you find healthy ways to cope.

Lessons Learned

It is important for me to be socially active and engage in meaningful work but it cannot be at the expense of my relationship with my family and wellbeing. I need to learn how to find balance in whatever I do making sure to prioritize my relationships and my activities.

Step back and consider...
...how many obligations fill your schedule.

Have you thought about.....

1. ...the pace of your life?
2. ...what is being thrown out of balance by living a life that is constantly on the go?
3. ...what changes will you make to regain balance in the different areas of your life?

5

Focus

I have always been a goal oriented individual, doing best when I have something to strive towards and focus on. Having just moved to Connecticut from Michigan and being a newlywed, new church youth group leader, new employee, new athlete and new friend to so many it was important for me to take time to focus in all of these different areas of my life. In order to focus, I took time to think through my goals for the different roles that I filled. Instead of generally wanting to be focused and succeed in the different areas, I articulated specifically what I would do to succeed. It became an annual practice where I would take time to think through each role I had and, using a goal journal, write down at least three goals in each area. I would come away knowing that I had set myself up for success and growth throughout the year in the different areas of my life.

Goals have become a very important part of my life and help me to stay focused. Let me encourage you to use goals in your own life. Goals help to provide clarity on whatever you want to accomplish. With a specific goal in mind, you can be assured that you are not spending time aimlessly achieving nothing. What you do on a daily basis takes you one day closer to achieving your dream. Having goals helps to motivate you and drive you forward when things get challenging. Instead of giving up, you are reminded of your focus with the goal ahead and are inspired to push through. When you have a focus and set goals, you are accountable.

There are many benefits to adopting goals. Goals obligate you to take action and make you accountable to yourself to follow through. Once you decide on a course of action, you want to stay true to your commitment. When faced with tough choices you are more apt to choose in alignment with your goals. Working towards goals helps you to achieve your highest potential. Goals force you to get out of your comfort zone and stretch yourself to new heights. With goals you can discover within yourself a determination and resiliency you did not know was there. You become more self-aware and learn new things about yourself. As you stretch yourself towards your goals, you are allowing yourself to get the best out of life. You are able to approach life with a new confidence and worldview to see the results of your focus.[9]

Lessons Learned

For me to be focused, I needed to create goals around the different roles in my life. I needed annual goals for myself as a Christian, wife, mother, sister, daughter, friend, business owner and athlete.

> *Step back and consider...*
> ...your existing list of goals.

Have you thought about.....

1. ...how goals can change your life?
2. ...what the main areas of your life to focus on are?
3. ...what you want to grow in each year?

6

Plastic

Since I was a young girl, I have always enjoyed drinking a lot of tea with cream and sugar. The tea I drank as an adult was consumed in a supersized plastic cup from a fast food restaurant. The cup was put in the microwave and used repeatedly until the structural integrity fell apart. I would throw away and replace the cup with another one if it showed signs of cracking or melted from overheating. The leftover food that I had after a meal was stored in plastic containers and then reheated in those plastic containers. My dry goods in the pantry were stored in plastic reusable containers. I used plastic containers for everything because they were cheap, convenient and so easy to find.

Inexpensive plastics have made many aspects of food and water distribution much easier but research and data suggest that we need to seriously consider our use of plastic.

Our health and the health of our planet would be in much better condition if we drastically reduced our use of plastic. Certain chemicals in plastics, like Bisphenol-A (BPA), are known to disrupt hormones and mimic the effect of estrogen in the body, leading to weight gain and hormone imbalance. BPA exposure has also been linked to premature puberty in females, decreased sperm quality, increases in breast and prostate cancers, infertility, miscarriages, obesity, type 2 diabetes, allergies and neurological problems, like attention deficit hyperactivity disorder. Plastics from food packaging can leach into the food we eat and enter the body. The Center for Disease Control reports that over 92% of people, including newborn babies, who were tested had detectable levels of BPA and other plastic chemicals in their bodies. Phthalates, another chemical found in plastics, are considered to be very harmful to men and boys, especially those exposed in utero. They are linked to immune system dysfunction, reduced testosterone levels, infertility in men and a host of other problems.[10]

The many chemicals in plastics are known endocrine disruptors. Plastics are considered to be safe by regulatory agencies, but it is not because they have been tested and proven to be safe for human use. In most cases, this means they have not been tested at all or that industry sponsored tests have shown them to be safe in small amounts.[10]

Here are some great ways to reduce plastic exposure in your life, the impact on the planet and save some money:

1) Start using a glass or stainless steel water bottle.
2) Switch to reusable grocery bags instead of plastic or paper bags.
3) Stop purchasing processed foods that have plastic packaging.

4) Shop at your local farmers market and use your own reusable bags.
5) Choose not to use or buy a plastic bag.
6) Replace your plastic bags and food storage containers with safer reusable options such as glass, stainless steel or silicon for storage.
7) Choose to buy wooden or metal toys for children as opposed to plastic.
8) Take your own glass or metal bottle when buying drinks away from home.
9) At home use glass and metal dishes, silverware and bakeware in place of plastic.
10) Recycle whatever you can![10]

Though plastic is ubiquitous we must explore healthier alternatives.

Lessons Learned

Plastics may be cheap and convenient but using them can have a negative impact on my health. The effects of plastic usage are long lasting and can be very damaging to my body and the environment.

Step back and consider...
...the plastic that surrounds you in your home.

Have you thought about.....

1. ...the amount of plastic used in your household?
2. ...how the plastic in your environment is affecting your health and that of your family?
3. ...what changes you will make to reduce the plastic around you?

7

Baseline Health

With the sugar, soda, processed food, hectic schedule and plastic in my life I was suffering from many health issues. I started to gain weight and was at a point where my clothes no longer fit comfortably. I suffered from migraine headaches that left me unable to function and led to dry heaving. At night I would often experience restless leg syndrome and have difficulty sleeping. My skin and nails were very dry and brittle. I felt disconnected from my husband because of my hectic schedule that kept me busy and away a lot. I did not have anything that I was taking time to do for myself in order to maintain balance and relieve stress. My amount of sleep decreased as I woke up early for work and stayed out late with the teens in the church youth group. The fast food, sugar and quick meals to exercise my body, never making it a priority in my schedule. My health deteriorated rapidly and I was not in a state of good health.

Good health is not defined as the absence of disease. It is a state of wellbeing that requires active participation on your part. There are several components to good health: physical health, mental health and spiritual health. Physical health or physical wellbeing is the one aspect of good health we likely think about most. Physical health usually involves having enough energy to do the tasks set before you, getting enough rest, eating the right kinds of foods, feeling well and feeling fit. The second component of good health is mental health. Mental health addresses our stress level, whether we enjoy life, and whether we are happy with who we are. The third component of good health is our spiritual health. Our spiritual health involves whether we are connected to God, feel at peace and feel we belong to something larger than ourselves.[11]

All of us have a role to play in achieving and maintaining good health. In order to become and stay healthy there are several things that we can actively do. It is important to eat a balanced diet that includes mainly organic fruits, vegetables, healthy fats and protein. There are many "diets" promoted but everyone must find a food lifestyle that works for them, given their specific needs.

Make time to exercise, get and stay active throughout the day. It is not enough to simply exercise in the morning for 30 minutes then be sedentary behind a desk for the rest of the day. Movement should take place every hour to stretch and keep the body active. Keep your weight in a good range by finding a food lifestyle and exercise routine that works best for you. Take time to research and experiment with different plans until you find one that best suits you.

Be careful about what you eat making sure it is organic, minimally processed and free from pesticides, herbicides, preservatives and hormones as often as possible. Shop the perimeter of the grocery store and visit the farmers market when possible to buy fresh foods that are in season and organic. Organize your daily schedule so that you get the optimal amount of sleep for your body. Everybody is unique but 7 to 8 hours of sleep is ideal for mental clarity and physical rejuvenation.

With the many challenges we face on a daily basis it is very important to find healthy ways to relieve stress. Some ways to relieve stress are fresh air, a work out, time with friends or yoga. Take time to unplug regularly and spend time with family and friends. Nurture your spirit by taking time to connect with God daily. Spend time praying and reading the Bible each day to maintain a healthy perspective. Get out in nature to see God's creation and take time to be grateful for all that you have. The final thing to help create and maintain good health is to find a primary care provider that is available to answer questions and help you annually with a checkup.

Lessons Learned

Though I was not fully aware of it, my body was telling me something was wrong and a change was necessary. It is important for me to be in touch with my body, mind and spirit and make sure I am in a state of good health and not simply existing. I must evaluate myself regularly and make changes as the need arises.

> *Step back and consider...*
> ...how in tune you are with your body.

Have you thought about.....

1. ...your current state of physical, mental and spiritual health?
2. ...which area of your health needs the most attention?
3. ...what changes will you make to be in a state of optimal health?

Part Two

WHERE ARE MY SNEAKERS?

8

Knowledge

When I was a newlywed I went out for a run with my husband. He had lost a lot of weight by running prior to our wedding and asked me to join him on a run. We went out together for a run around the block but I was quickly winded and finished the time out walking. I concluded that I was not a runner and we did not go out together again. A couple of years later a friend asked me to join her team of 3 in an adventure race. An adventure race involved trail running, mountain biking, canoeing and navigating with a map and compass. The distances for each could range from 3 to 10 miles and take 5 or more hours to complete. I was perplexed by her request to join her knowing that I was not a runner or biker and did not exercise regularly. I accepted her offer because she was my friend but I let her know that I was starting at ground zero and would have to learn everything from the beginning. That is where the training and my life as an athlete began.

In order to be a contributing member of the race team I needed to get in shape and learn all I could in order to participate successfully. We started training to develop endurance for the running. Next we moved onto the bike and riding on trails. Finally we worked on the physical strength to scale a wall as that would be one of the obstacles we were going to face as part of the race. As we trained I learned a lot about myself and the different sports. I learned that I am determined, focused, consistent and capable. Up until this point in my life I had not put this much focused energy into any sport.

Any pursuit in life requires knowledge. Knowledge of where you are and where you want to go. It is important to take time to get to know yourself as it relates to the task at hand. In becoming an athlete consider your current physical condition and what is needed to perform successfully. Read books and articles that talk about and lay out a weekly workout schedule that starts at your current fitness level. Whether couch to 5K or setting a new personal best completing a marathon or Ironman triathlon, there are many training plan options available. Look at your diet, consider whether the foods you currently eat allow you to perform at your best or are they a hindrance. Learn about pre- and post-workout meals that help you during the activity and help you recover quickly afterwards. What you learn may require you to overhaul your diet in order to see the success you want.

Take time to research the necessary training and racing gear. Running requires a good pair of running shoes that give you the foot support and stability you need. Purchase running shoes from your local running store where the sales people are runners themselves and know best how to direct you. The wrong shoe will not only prevent you from doing well but can also lead to injury. While at the running store learn about and purchase clothing that is made of wicking material that will keep the moisture of sweat away from your body. If you plan to run in the winter, learn about the running shell that will keep the wind and rain off you and keep you warm when you head outdoors. If you want to run indoors, is there a local gym or YMCA you can join or consider if you want to invest in a treadmill for your home.

If you are taking up biking, read bike reviews to find the bike that best fits your body and your price range. Once you have purchased a bike, learn how to maintain it and change a flat tire when necessary. Take time to understand the laws for riding on the road. If you are interested in swimming, the local YMCA provides a great environment and offers swim lessons at a variety of levels. As with running, purchase your swimming equipment such as goggles, swim suit and flippers from a store that sells to local swim teams. Find out about and incorporate a strength routine to develop muscle and the power necessary for your sport of interest. Learn how to stretch your body correctly for each sport to avoid injury.

Talk to people or look up reviews from individuals who have completed the event you are interested in beforehand in order to get an idea of how to prepare yourself. Go to the event website and look at the different details they provide in order to make sure you know what will be available on site and what you need to plan to take with you. Drive over the racecourse prior to the event to familiarize yourself with where you will be going and the terrain you will be covering.

Stay aware of the weather on the day of the event so you can best plan on what to wear for the race. You will need to plan ahead and dress appropriately for the time before the race while you wait for it to start and for the ride home once it is over. If the event is an Olympic triathlon, half marathon or longer, learn about the fuel needed during the race for sustained energy. Take time during training to determine which of the fuel sources works best for you. Purchase different energy gels, beverages or make your own to find one you like. Learn about the suggested recovery time after your race, working out too soon after an event can lead to injury.

Lessons learned

Attempting a new sport is great but it is necessary for me to take the time to learn as much as I can in order to succeed. I need to be patient with my current level of fitness and train to get to a level that allows me to complete the event successfully and injury free.

Step back and consider...
    ...your eagerness to learn about something new.

Have you thought about.....

1. ...what you currently know about an activity or goal you want to pursue?
2. ...what kind of character traits or equipment you will need to reach your goal?
3. ...what changes you will need to make in your life to attain your goal?

9

Exercise

After the adventure race I completed with my friends, my mud covered sneakers sat on the doormat until the following April. I had successfully completed the race and really enjoyed everything about it. What I realized as I trained for the adventure race was that I enjoyed being physically active, I enjoyed using the muscles in my body to propel me forward. Since the running bug had bit me, I started running as soon as Spring hit. My friend and I identified and began training for upcoming races. We started the year with a 5K road race and ended it with a half marathon. By the end of the year I had completed several road races, developed my endurance and running pace. In the years that followed I added biking and swimming to my exercise routine and completed many triathlons with dreams of completing an Ironman race. I had never seen myself as an athlete or someone that exercised regularly but here I was doing just that. My life was redefined as exercise took on a large part of it and my body benefited from it in many ways. I no longer suffered from restless legs, my migraine headaches subsided, I lost weight and started drinking water regularly.

There are several ways that regular exercise can benefit you. Exercise can help prevent excess weight gain or help maintain weight loss. When you engage in physical activity, you burn calories. The more intense the activity, the more calories you burn. Large amounts of time for exercise are not necessary to reap weight-loss benefits. If you can't do an actual workout, get more active throughout the day by taking the stairs instead of the elevator, speeding up your household chores, going for a walk or parking further from the store. No matter what your current weight, being active increases high-density lipoprotein (HDL), or "good" cholesterol and decreases unhealthy triglycerides.

Exercise keeps your blood flowing smoothly, which decreases your risk of cardiovascular diseases. Regular physical activity can help you prevent, as well as manage, a wide range of health issues and concerns, including stroke, metabolic syndrome, type 2 diabetes, depression, certain types of cancer, arthritis and can strengthen your body to minimize falls. Also, exercise stimulates various brain chemicals that leave you feeling happier and more relaxed. When you exercise regularly you also feel better about your appearance and yourself, which boosts your confidence and improves your self-esteem. Regular physical activity can improve your strength and increase your endurance. Exercise and physical activity deliver oxygen and nutrients to your tissues and help your cardiovascular system work more efficiently. When your heart and lungs work more efficiently, you have more energy to go about your daily responsibilities. Regular physical activity can improve the quality of your sleep by helping you fall asleep faster and deepen your sleep. Exercise and physical activity give you a chance to unwind, enjoy the outdoors or engage in activities that make you happy. Physical activity can also help you connect with family or friends in a fun social setting. Take time to find a physical activity you enjoy, and commit to doing it regularly.[12]

As a general goal, engage in at least 30 minutes of physical activity every day. If you want to lose weight or meet specific fitness goals for a race, you may need to exercise for a longer period of time.

It is very important to check with your doctor before starting a new exercise program, especially if you haven't exercised for a long time, have chronic health problems, such as heart disease, diabetes or arthritis, or if you have any other concerns.

Lessons Learned

Exercise is important for me physically and psychologically. I need to exercise regularly to feel balanced. When I don't exercise, my mind is unsettled and anxious, my body becomes unfit and stagnant.

Step back and consider...
...how much you move throughout the day.

Have you thought about.....

1. ...your current level of exercise?
2. ...how your health can be improved by exercising regularly?
3. ...what you can do to incorporate more exercise into your life?

10
Nutrition

As I trained for the different road races and triathlons I realized that I had to modify my eating habits. My food choices included a lot of sugar, processed food, fast food and little to no vegetables. I needed to find an eating lifestyle—not a diet—that would help me to perform at my best level. I wanted to find an eating plan that I could enjoy throughout my life and not feel deprived while giving my body the essential nutrients that it needs. The search began to find a long-term sustainable solution.

As Americans, we're a little obsessed with our weight and spend a good amount of time paying attention to the latest diet fads. Companies spend millions and millions of dollars luring us to try the latest diet with promises that this will be the solution, our shortcut to a skinny figure. Studies show that due to advertising and examples from other women in their lives young girls are starting diets as early as ages 8 or 9.

While diets can work for a while, most often they end up failing. There are several reasons why diets fail. Each person is a unique individual with different requirements for maintaining a healthy body. There are many factors that affect what a person's body needs, including gender, age, ancestry and lifestyle. While a diet might seem to be successful for a while, research now proves that almost all diets result in a 10-pound gain. Diets don't work because they are too restrictive for the average person. It is unhealthy to restrict, deprive and control the body at levels most diets dictate. Diets really take us away from our own inner wisdom, our common sense that tells us what to eat, when to eat and when to sleep. When you begin to listen to your own unique body you will find what gives it energy, what stabilizes your weight and what creates lasting health.

In my quest to find the best eating lifestyle for me I looked at the various diets that are being promoted and gleaned something from them to create the best plan for me.

- The Atkins Diet is a low carbohydrate diet that emphasizes proteins and fats, based on the assumption that the body will switch its metabolic burning process from sugar to fat burning.

- The South Beach diet focuses on "good" carbohydrates and "good" fats.

- The Zone diet focuses on a balance between protein, carbohydrates and fats based on a 40:30:30 ratio.

- The Vegetarian diet excludes animal products including meat, poultry, and fish. The emphasis is on a plant-based diet.

- Vegan diet excludes consumption of meat, poultry, fish and all animal products including eggs, dairy and honey.

- The Macrobiotic diet is traditionally a Japanese diet that calls for local, fresh and unrefined foods consisting mostly of grains, vegetables and beans.

- The Ayurveda diet is based on the ancient Indian science of Ayurvedic medicine that looks at specific doshas (body types) and describes foods that will enhance or detract from health for each body type.

- The Mediterranean diet consists of whole grains, fish, meat or poultry in small portions and lots of fresh vegetables.

- The Raw Food diet promotes uncooked foods and consists largely of fruits, vegetables, nuts, seeds and other raw foods including fish, meat, eggs, and dairy.

- The Intuitive Eating diet is the practice of learning to listen to your body's signals in order to eat properly, instead of focusing on counting calories.

- A Gluten Free diet eliminates gluten, which is found in products containing wheat, barley, rye, oats and triticale.

There are many diet plans out there and it is critical that you take the time to experiment with the different ideas and find an eating lifestyle that works best for you. Make sure that the plan you settle on, or combination of the above, includes the macronutrients, carbohydrates, fats, proteins, and the micronutrients, vitamins, minerals, antioxidants and fiber to support optimal health and real nourishment for you.

Real nourishment comes from foods and activities that feed your body and soul in a way that creates additional energy. Sugar and caffeine, the two items most commonly relied on for quick energy actually have the opposite effect. Sugar and caffeine initially provide us with the desired energy boost but as they are processed in the body they send us crashing. In order to have sustained energy choose water instead of energy drinks and beverages filled with caffeine and sugar, eat green vegetables that cleanse the body, include lots of healthy fats and take time to relax your body and mind. As you incorporate nourishing foods you will experience sustained energy and find that your cravings for some of the unhealthier foods will diminish as they get crowded out.[13]

Lessons Learned

A healthy balanced diet is imperative for my wellbeing. I needed to take all the information I had gathered and create an eating lifestyle that supported my unique self. Fad diets come and go, I needed a plan that was effective and sustainable. The plan needed to consider my body, level of activity and family. What works best for me, giving me sustained energy and optimal health, is a plan that includes a high amount of healthy fats, a moderate amount of protein and a low level of carbohydrates.

Step back and consider...
...if you are truly being nourished daily.

Have you thought about.....

1. ...whether your current food choices provide you with optimal nourishment?
2. ...which eating plan will help give you sustained energy?
3. ...what changes you will make to your current eating plan?

11

Self-Care

After having my first child in 2007 my life took on a different dimension. My husband and I decided to stop leading the youth group at church so we could focus on our growing family. I stayed at home with my new daughter for six months then returned to fulltime work. The time at home gave me a great opportunity to connect with my daughter and adjust to being a first time mother. Once I returned to work things were very hectic as I juggled my schedule between the family, relationships, church, training for races and work.

When my daughter was one my husband, a chemist, changed careers and went back to school to become a pharmacist, further complicating things. With my husband's new focus as a student he spent long hours away from the house studying. As he was working on his new career I found myself working very hard to take care of the house, care for our daughter, connect with my husband, train for races and represent the family at social activities. At first I was able to fill this new role with enthusiasm, doing what needed to be done. As time went on I could see that my daughter and husband were happy and thriving but I was not. I found myself becoming increasingly unhappy even though my household was doing well. When I sat down to think about why I was feeling discouraged, resentful, and burned out I realized it was because I was not taking time for myself. I was so busy taking care of my family that I was not taking care of my own well-being. I was not taking time out to meet my own needs and manage the stress I was experiencing.

Self-care is essential in order to live a balanced life. When we neglect our own needs we risk deep levels of unhappiness, low self-esteem and start experiencing feelings of resentment. When our own needs are not met in the midst of a busy schedule, we get burned out and are no longer effective at meeting the needs of those in our care. Often times we play the role of the martyr by meeting the needs of our family, community, relationships, jobs and pets at the expense of our own peace and wellbeing. It is important to take time to do the different activities that encourage you. A balance must be found between the stress of life and activities that bring you peace. Make time to figure out what would bring you peace, maybe it is a massage regularly, a night out with the girls, time to just sit and read, painting, journaling, taking a nap, taking an interesting class, meditation or engaging in some exercise.[14]

Once you have identified what will help you reenergize, communicate it to your loved ones. Let them know what you are feeling and that this time you take for self-care will allow you to serve them better as you will be doing so in a more peaceful, joyful state. At first you might feel guilty for taking time out for yourself but over time you will see and feel the difference as your attitude, productivity and mood change. The temptation might be to take time out for a while then go back to the life of a martyr but to do so does everyone a disservice. Your self-care should be a regular ongoing part of your schedule. Your interests may change over time but you must always make time for them realizing their importance in your life.

Lessons Learned

There is always something to do and something going on in our hectic, fast-paced lives. It is essential that I take time for myself to recharge and meet my personal needs. If I do not take time for myself, I will not be able to successfully give to others without burnout, overwhelm and resentment.

Step back and consider...
...how refreshed and at peace you feel.

Have you thought about.....

1. ...when you last took time out for yourself?
2. ...how much better you could serve your loved ones if you took time out for self-care?
3. ...what activities you will engage in regularly to maintain a sense of peace and balance?

12

Sleep

As I trained for triathlons and road races, worked with the youth group, developed my relationship with my husband and had a career, I felt I had little time to get adequate sleep. Some mornings I would get up at 3:30 to train on my stationary bike after having stayed up late talking to my husband when I got home from being out with the teens in our church. My sleep was sacrificed in order to accomplish the goals I had laid out. Growing up I always needed and got a lot of sleep but when I became an adult, sleep was the first to go in the interest of productivity. I forgot how critical sleep is to a balanced life and often only got five hours of sleep. Dismissing adequate sleep left me exhausted, unable to think clearly and very easily frustrated. Looking to find balance, I decided to prioritize my sleep and better understand the impact of not getting enough.

Most people need seven to eight, sometimes more, hours of sleep to function optimally. A lack of sleep has been linked to a wide variety of health problems. One problem that results from getting inadequate sleep is weight gain. When you do not get enough sleep your appetite-inducing hormone, ghrelin, is increased causing you to eat more. The later you stay up the more food you will naturally consume leading to weight gain. Another problem associated with a reduced amount of sleep is the inability to think clearly that leads to an increase in the number of accidents seen on the road and at home. Depression also results from insomnia and sleep apnoea. Chronic diseases such as diabetes, decreased immune function, cardiovascular and heart disease, Alzheimer's and cancer can all result from prolonged sleep deprivation as it compromises the body's ability to function optimally.[15]

It is important to prioritize sleep in order to live a balanced, healthy life. Determine the appropriate amount of sleep that your body needs then implement some habits to ensure you get the rest your body needs. To determine how much sleep you need wake up naturally without an alarm and see how many hours it takes you to wake up on your own feeling rested and refreshed. The amount of sleep necessary varies from person to person, it is important to consider your own unique needs. The first habit is to establish and stick to a sleep schedule that allows you to go to bed and wake up at the same time every day of the week. Once your schedule is in place create a bedtime routine that helps you relax and unwind helping your body to fall asleep faster. If you have trouble getting to sleep at night avoiding a power nap during the day is helpful. Caffeine and other stimulants should be avoided too close to bedtime, as they will negatively impact your ability to get to sleep.[16] In order to calm your racing thoughts keep a note book by the side of your bed and jot things down so your mind is at peace and able to rest. Daily exercise, even if it is light, is a great way to release anxious energy and help you relax when it is time to sleep. Another great habit is to make sure that the room you sleep in is not too hot, a cool room creates a better sleep environment. As much as possible try to eliminate noisy distractions and bright lights that can interfere with deep, restorative sleep. When it comes to what you sleep on, buy a pillow and mattress that are comfortable and supportive for your body. The surface you sleep on can have a significant impact on the quality of sleep you get each night.[17]

Lessons Learned

No matter how busy my days get I must always make time to get adequate sleep even if certain things do not get done. In order to function optimally I must prioritize sleep and make sure I create the most conducive environment.

Step back and consider...
...how many hours sleep you got each night last week.

Have you thought about.....

1. ...whether you are getting an adequate amount of sleep each night?
2. ...how is your life affected by the amount of sleep you get?
3. ...what you can do to improve the duration and quality of your sleep?

13

Discipline

In order to succeed at living a balanced life that included time to gain knowledge, time to exercise sufficiently, a healthy eating lifestyle, a plan for self-care and adequate sleep I needed to be very disciplined. No goal or great achievement is reached without discipline. It becomes the number one trait you need to help you excel. Discipline is the ability to control your emotions, wants and desires now in order to experience the long-term success of reaching your goal in the future. Being disciplined is being able to set goals and act on them no matter how challenging things get along the way. Living a disciplined life does not mean giving up what you enjoy but it does mean being able to focus on your goals and what you need to do to accomplish them. Self-discipline also means making focused deliberate choices and not giving way to emotions and bad habits.[18]

The discipline necessary to live a balanced life achieving your goals can be developed over time.

In your pursuit of discipline you need to determine what inspires and drives you, also what challenges you when things get hard. Do what you can to create an environment that will push you towards your goal not detract you. Once you have determined your goals put certain habits in place that you will do daily to move you closer towards your goal. Take the larger goal and break it down into smaller daily actionable steps. Actions done daily as part of a habit will help you build self-discipline. As you work on developing certain habits learn to pause and say no to different thoughts you have that will derail you from your goal. Ask yourself if the choice you are faced with will move you closer to or further away from your goal. The more times you say no, the more in control things remain. Developing discipline will help you to avoid acting on impulse, fulfill your promises to yourself and others, not give in to laziness, persevere through tough times, follow through on projects, get up early and avoid engaging in activities that waste time.[19]

As I trained for running road races and triathlons, I became more and more disciplined over all. I was able to take the discipline I learned in training and apply it to other areas of my life. I found myself being able to push and challenge myself to do things I had not previously had the confidence or self-control to do.

Lessons Learned

Having goals is important for me and the only way for me to reach them is to live a very disciplined life. I must be willing to get up very early before the family and be willing to say no to activities that will derail my plans. I must be willing to say no to foods that will impact my body in a negative way. Once a training plan is set it must be followed to complete the race successfully.

> *Step back and consider...*
>   ...the barriers in your life that prevent you
>   from reaching your goals.

Have you thought about.....

1. ...how disciplined you are in reaching your goals?
2. ...the areas of your life where you need to be more disciplined?
3. ...what habits you can develop to help you be more disciplined in reaching your goals?

14

Community

While growing up on the campus of Bunda College of Agriculture in Malawi, Central Africa, families came together often to spend time with each other and share a meal. As a result, I learned to love and appreciate being part of a rich community. As a runner I participated in different races throughout the years; I was drawn to and became part of the running and triathlon community. My experiences in the events were greatly enriched when I saw myself as a part of the community. I enjoyed seeing familiar faces year after year and the post-race festivities were spent connecting with friends and talking about the race.

There are many benefits to becoming a part of a community as you engage in running, triathlon or any other sport. You will meet like-minded individuals that share your passion. You'll receive coaching, motivation, advice and guidance from fellow athletes. More experienced athletes will be able to motivate you past 'the wall'. As a member of the community you will be able to help others with the knowledge you have gained in your own training and racing. You can take part in races as a group instead of doing it alone. You can share your achievements with others that can understand and relate. In the community you will meet a whole group of people with whom you can compare stats, times and even your latest gadgets. As part of the community you may be more likely to continue the sport. Communication within the group will help you stay aware of the latest running events, product reviews, recommendations, techniques, best practices and news. You can always find a fellow member with whom to go out and exercise. Through the community you will learn about, and maybe even take part in, other sports. You will learn how other people manage their time and nutrition, providing you with useful tips for your own training. Some of the people you meet will become lifelong friends. You will be introduced to a whole new social circle that you would not have otherwise met. You'll feel more inspired and motivated to get out there and train.

If you don't know many people in the area, running clubs and sports teams offer a great way of introducing yourself to local residents. A good running club can help you de-stress after a long day of work or study. Individuals can provide helpful correction on your technique. You'll be able to try out a variety of local routes and even incorporate them into your own training. Training as part of a community will help you spend more time outdoors and less time in the gym. You will be able to progress along with other fellow runners and look back together on your achievements.[20]

Lessons Learned

Community and a sense of belonging is very important to me. I enjoy being around like-minded people that share my interests and passions. It is important to find my community around the different goals I have as it helps me feel energized and succeed.

Step back and consider...
...who is part of your community.

Have you thought about.....

1. ...how important community is to you?
2. ...which communities you could get involved in?
3. ...how different your experience would be if you participated in an activity as part of a community?

Part Three

LIFE CAN BE SIMPLE

15

Gratitude

As I entered the next phase of my life I was left with a sense of gratitude for all the things I was experiencing and learning. I was grateful for my improved health free of migraines, restless legs and other health issues that had previously plagued me. I was grateful for the new active lifestyle, running and triathlon community that were now a part of my life. The changes in my nutrition left me feeling grateful for improved health and the energy to do the things I wanted. Developing discipline left me feeling grateful to have a trait that would help me reach my goals. Prioritizing sleep gave me a sense of gratitude, as I was now able to approach each day refreshed and energized. The gratitude I was experiencing gave me a sense of peace and happiness that had eluded me when I was not working towards a balanced life. Aside from what I was experiencing due to gratitude, the books I read helped reinforce the fact that it is critical for me to maintain a sense of gratitude in my life.

Being grateful is taking time to be thankful and consider all of the blessings you have been given. Looking at your life and seeing all of the things you have, not what you do not have, is important. Individuals who consciously focus on being grateful, experience better emotional and physical health than those who do not. Cultivating a perspective of gratitude may help you:

1) Feel better about your life
2) Experience more joy and happiness
3) Feel more optimistic about the future
4) Strengthen your immune system
5) Exercise more often
6) Have more energy
7) Make progress towards goals
8) Sleep better
9) Reduce your stress
10) Be more creative[21]

Maintaining a sense of gratitude will help you remain happier regardless of the circumstances around you. Take time to find joy and be grateful for the little things you experience daily.[22]

There are several ways to create a practice of gratitude on a regular basis. At the beginning or end of each day take a few minutes and write down five things for which you are grateful. Give thank you cards to different people in your life that have positively impacted you.[23] Carry or wear something that will remind you of the many blessings you have.[22] When you sit down for dinner with your family have each person say three things they are grateful for about the day. Take time regularly to pray a prayer of gratitude, not asking for anything but just being grateful for all that you have. Look for the good in situations and people; we see what we focus on. Take a walk outside and just allow yourself to take in nature, be grateful for all that you see and experience. When you are in the midst of a challenging time consider the fact that things could be worse. Look back at the difficult times you faced and think about how you have grown and the good that came from them. Take time out of your schedule to volunteer in your community, it will help you be grateful for all you have. Surround yourself with people who are grateful, as they will help you see things to be grateful for in your life.[23]

Lessons Learned

It is very important that I maintain a perspective of gratitude. Developing and maintaining a practice of gratitude only takes a few minutes out of each day but it has lasting results.

Step back and consider...
...all that you have around you.

Have you thought about…..

1. …why you are grateful?
2. …whether you have a gratitude practice?
3. …what will you do regularly to cultivate gratitude in your life?

16

Coaching

The first 13 years of my life as a runner and triathlete I was self-coached. I had a friend with whom I travelled to races but what I learned I taught myself. I am a voracious reader and would read any article or book on swimming, biking and running on which I could get my hands. I enjoyed taking the information I learned and applying it to my training. As time progressed, I saw improvements in my running times and could see myself growing as a triathlete. After seeing the Hawaii Ironman Race, my dream became to one day compete in the race. With my ironman dream in mind, I knew I had to move beyond the sprint distance triathlons and half marathons in which I regularly competed. I set my sights on a half ironman and read all I could in order to train adequately for the distance. The half Ironman race took all aspects of my training to a whole new level. On race day I stood at the start line ready to embark on the next phase of my goal. I had a great race, completing it in eight and a half hours. I was very happy with my performance having challenged myself and pushed my body to the limit. After the race, I planned for my next half Ironman race and realized that in order to reach my goal I would need to complete it in under eight hours and make all of the cut off times for each leg of the race. I had successfully coached myself to this point but also knew that to take it to the next level I needed to hire a coach.

When hiring a coach, it is important to consider more than just their credentials. When you meet them for the first time consider your first impression and if a connection was made. As you sit down for your introductory session there should be mutual respect present. The coach should have an exercise and nutritional approach that considers your specific needs and what will help you reach your goals. The approach used should be part of the coach's unique philosophy and not simply a plan that they incorporated and followed from someone else. If things are not working out with the coach they should care enough to point you in a direction where you will find the best fit. The education that a coach has is important, but they must be able to use that knowledge appropriately to help you reach your goal. It is not enough to know the material; they must be able to apply it to your unique situation. Flexibility is very important in a coach, as they need to be able to adapt to the needs of each session and not stick too rigidly to a prepared script.[24]

Hiring a coach can make the world of difference when it comes to planning workouts and staying motivated. I knew how to plan a workout schedule but my coach helped me with the fine balance of hard workouts and rest days and my nutrition plan for training and racing.[25] A good coach knows how hard to push you given their level of experience. My coach took the time necessary to put together a complete plan, time I did not always have. Accountability for the training comes with the coach, otherwise it might be all too easy to skip a workout.[26] You are less likely to forgo a workout if you know your coach will ask you about it. I had learned a fair amount over the years but my coach knew more than I did when it came to physiology, strength training and the mechanics of running, biking and swimming. My coach and I developed a partnership that worked to help me succeed in the pursuit of my goals. We worked very closely to make sure I started each race in peak condition. She supported me throughout the process of training which included driving me to the racecourse to familiarize me with the terrain and course layout.

Lessons Learned

Having a coach proved to be very beneficial in helping me make improvements and reach my goals. My coach knew more about a balanced exercise plan than I did and was able to help me incorporate things into training that I had not considered. Having a coach is very helpful for focus and accountability.

Step back and consider...
...who plays the role of a coach in your life.

Have you thought about…..

1. …how you can benefit from a coach?
2. …which areas of your life, if not exercise, could use additional support and accountability?
3. …which of your goals could become a reality with the help of a coach?

17

Helping Others

As I continued to pursue my goals of a healthy and balanced lifestyle, I talked to my friends and others around me about what I was doing. I shared about the transformation that I had undergone and the steps I took towards health and balance. The more I talked to people the more I saw that there are many women who share my passion and dream.

A lot of women want to live lives that are healthy and balanced in the midst of a very hectic schedule. The challenge, that women seeking change face, is they do not know where to start. They find themselves overwhelmed with all the nutrition and exercise information that is available. To create a framework for change I worked with some women in my church and helped put together a series of 7 workshops that were designed to be informational and supportive. The workshops took place every other week and covered different topics such as exercise, stretching, healthy eating and healthy aging. Throughout the series every participant had an accountability partner with a similar goal. The women would encourage and support each other as they pursued their goals. Each workshop was well received and the participants were able to make impactful changes in their lives. The woman came away with the tools and information necessary to successfully complete their goals. In addition to presenting a workshop I held a cooking demonstration that taught the participants how to cook a complete and balanced meal from scratch using healthy ingredients.

My experience presenting the workshops and the cooking demonstration showed me that I enjoyed sharing what I have learned and that there is a need to help others. There are a lot of women in the same situation that I was in, they want to make a change in their life, but do not know where to start and do not have the support to do so.

Understanding how much I had benefited from a coach I decided to go to school to get my Wellness Coaching certification. I wanted the opportunity to make a difference in the lives of women around me. The program I studied was holistic in nature and approached health from many different areas. Instead of focusing solely on nutrition for wellbeing and balance we looked at sleep, exercise, relationships, work satisfaction, play and spirituality realizing they all play a role in a healthy lifestyle. I wanted to help women in the most balanced way possible understanding that an imbalance in one area of life can manifest itself in another area.

As I went through the certification program, I was a coaching client myself and saw firsthand the type of impact that holistic coaching can have. With the help of my coach I was able to find balance with my exercise, self-care and family commitments. I came away from the program very excited to be able to help busy women find balance in their lives because they are facing burn out and are overwhelmed. I want to provide the solution that many women are looking for in a hectic, fast-paced life.

Lessons Learned

Realizing how much I know and have benefited from coaching it is important for me to give back and help others in a similar situation. I do a huge disservice if I do not help others reach their health and balance goals.

Step back and consider...
   ...what you have learned from the help
   you received.

Have you thought about.....

1. ...how you can help others with what you know?
2. ...who you know that is in a position that could use your help?
3. ...the difference you will make in someone's life by sharing what you know?

18
Family

My family has always been very important to me. Growing up my mother did an amazing job instilling a sense of family in my siblings and me. We had meals together daily, went on family vacations together, talked often, played games together, cooked together, and supported each other's interests and milestones. When I got married and then later had a child, it was very important to me that I create a sense of family with them too.

Creating a sense of family involves spending quality time together, which can have a lasting impact on children. Quality time creates a stronger emotional bond between the parents and the children. Communication within the family is better when the relationship is strengthened. Children who have better communication with their parents perform better in school and have fewer behavioral challenges. With a strong bond between parent and child, children are able to "open up" about their lives and work through the tough times they face. Family time leaves children feeling happier and in better emotional health. More time and attention from adults helps children develop a healthy outlook on life so they will not feel the need to engage in negative behavior to get attention.[27]

A sense of family can be developed by participating in a variety of activities together. Some activities that build family are volunteering in the community, cooking family meals, eating meals together, spending time talking and sharing dreams, attending sporting games, running errands, playing board games, hiking, day trips, morning and bedtime routines, attending social activities together, gardening, and maintaining the home by doing chores together. [27] Since life can get very hectic at times the various activities should be scheduled into the week for them to happen consistently.

Early in our marriage, I worked to create a sense of family with meals and shared activities, which were sometimes successful and sometimes not so successful. My husband and I had differing perspectives on family, having had different childhood experiences. Up until having our first child, I still did things independently not always involving my husband even though I wanted to create a sense of family. When I had my first child, I continued to pursue creating a sense of family and even more so as our family was growing. I sought out ways to create family both inside and outside the home. Inside the home I made sure we had meals together and created bonding routines in the morning and evening. Outside the home I created family volunteering in the community and around the races in which I participated. I invited my husband to train and race with me. My husband completed a half marathon and two eight hour, grueling adventure races with me. Our experience with adventure racing led to a very well received and enjoyable adventure race that we created for our church youth camp. Organizing the event and working on the details together was very gratifying.

After those shared experiences we came away feeling more connected and unified with each other. While training at the track for races, my daughter would come with me and play on the nearby playground. When the race in which I participated had a kid's race, I signed my daughter up for it. She took great pleasure in "training" with me and receiving a medal like mine after her race. I had an extra fuel belt for her in which she put candy and gummy bears. We traveled to out of town races together and created memories spending the night in the hotel. When I completed my half Ironman races, my daughter and husband spent the day playing on the beach and cheering me on during the transition. We were able to share in that time together and come away feeling closer. Even when my family cannot attend a race with me, I feel supported by my husband who watches the children. Racing is an activity in which we still participate and build family memories.

Lessons Learned

It is important to find ways to include my family in what I do and create a sense of family. I have individual goals, however, it is important for my goals not to affect my relationship with my family.

Step back and consider...
...those you hold most dear.

Have you thought about.....

1. ...what family means to you?
2. ...how to create a sense of family with your loved ones?
3. ...the long lasting impact of creating family?

19

Homemade Food

The more I trained for running and triathlon races the healthier I wanted to be. I realized that my weekly training would get me to a certain level of fitness but in order to function optimally I needed to watch the food that I ate even more closely. Having grown up eating homemade meals and appreciating all my mother did I decided to learn how to cook my own meals. The foods I ate were minimally processed but processed none the less. I searched the internet to find recipes for the foods I regularly ate and prepared for my family. In doing so, I felt better physically and my performance started to improve.

Cooking what you eat at home allows you to control the ingredients in your food, whereas, you can use natural, fresh ingredients instead of unhealthy ones. Processed foods, frequently served in restaurants or available in premade meals from the grocery store, are high in sodium, unhealthy fats and added sugars. Eating homemade foods lets you add more fresh fruits and vegetables to your meals so that you can focus on all-natural ingredients. Home cooking also allows you to control the amount of sodium and sugar you eat with every meal. You can use healthier cooking methods, such as, baking instead of frying, substituting healthy ingredients for unhealthy ingredients, using butter instead of vegetable oil, when making your own meals.

Cooking at home is cheaper than going to a restaurant or buying pre-cooked meals. When you eat at home you are able to control your portion size and reduce the urge to indulge by eating oversized restaurant portions. Eating at home often includes more fruits and vegetables and teaches the whole family about good nutrition that leads to a healthier lifestyle. When meals are prepared at home, you are better able to accommodate family members with allergies to such things as peanuts, dairy and shellfish. You are also able to protect your family from exposure to the protein gluten found in the seeds of grasses such as wheat, barley, oats, rye and rice. Exposure to gluten can lead to an autoimmune response in some individuals.[28] Cooking at home using less sugar and salt will help to re-sensitize your palate making food more flavorful and enjoyable.

Cooking and sharing a meal together at home provides great opportunities for communication and connection that might otherwise not happen in a family. Involving children in food preparation is an amazing way to teach them about healthy eating habits. Statistically, children who grow up in households where meals are eaten together perform better academically and show less tendency toward engaging in risky behaviors such as smoking, drinking and taking drugs, according to Washington State University nutrition researchers Martha Marina and Sue Butkus.[29]

Lessons Learned

I really enjoy cooking my own food. It is very important to me that I know what goes into the food I eat. Spending time in the kitchen is worth it to ensure healthy, better tasting food and the improved health of my family. Our kitchen has become a place of great significance as our family spends time together preparing a meal we will later sit down and enjoy eating.

Step back and consider...
...the last meal you cooked and enjoyed with your family.

Have you thought about.....

1. ...the different ingredients in the processed foods you eat?
2. ...how the health of the family will improve by eating homemade meals?
3. ...the impact on your children long term when you cook and eat at home.

20

Garden

Having grown up with a garden and appreciating fresh vegetables as a child, a garden of my own was the next step in the journey towards health. As my eating pattern had changed and now included organic fruits and vegetables, I wanted to try growing what we purchased. My husband and I determined where in our yard the garden would be, making sure that what we grew received plenty of direct sun light. We decided to grow carrots, corn, cabbage, pumpkins, cucumbers, onion and tomatoes. This being our first garden my husband and I did some research to make sure things were planted, grown, weeded and harvested correctly. I found the information we were looking for and also discovered a lot of benefits beyond nutrition when it comes to having a garden.

Some of the reasons to garden are stress reduction, exercise, brain health, healing and immunity. A research study conducted in the Netherlands concluded that gardening is a better stress reliever than some relaxing leisure activities. The improved level of stress can reduce the incidents of headaches, irritability, stomach aches and heart attacks.

Gardening involves the whole body in physical activity. The regular physical activity of gardening done for two and a half hours a week can help prevent heart disease, high blood pressure, obesity, adult-onset diabetes, depression, colon cancer and osteoporosis. Gardening on a regular bases was found to help lower the risk of dementia by 36% in older adults. Gardening requires you to think and be creative, using your mind in this way helps to guard you against degenerative diseases. There is strong evidence, discovered by Roger S. Ulrich, that being in nature helps our bodies heal better and faster. Researcher Christopher Lowry found that certain soil bacteria stimulated the immune system and made it stronger. Some experts say that being in the fresh air while gardening can help prevent Attention Deficit Hyperactivity Disorder and lead to improvements as a student.[30]

Individuals who garden tend to have a more positive outlook on life. Gardening gives us an opportunity to observe and learn from nature, forcing us to slow down and step out of our hectic lives. The tastes, scents, colors, textures and sounds we experience in a garden allow us to engage all of our senses. [31] A garden is an important part of the ecosystem that supports bees and other beneficial insects. Composting household vegetable and fruit scraps is a great way to recycle waste and create nutrient rich soil to fertilize your garden. A garden does not require a lot of land—vegetables can be grown in buckets on the deck or porch allowing the gardener to experience all the benefits of a full garden.

Having a young daughter at the time of our first garden I wanted her to experience planting, caring for and eating food fresh from our garden. It was important that she understand where her food comes from and also reap the many benefits and lessons from growing up with a garden. When children participate in gardening they learn to be more responsible as they take care of the plants. As children learn to be more responsible they learn the lessons of cause and effect. They start to realize that if certain things are not done, such as watering, there are consequences—the plants will die. As the plants grow and thrive children develop self-confidence as they reach the goal of harvesting and eating what they planted. Spending time outside can help children learn how to appreciate nature and the beauty that surrounds them. They will experience and start to understand the ebb and flow of nature as they watch the garden grow. As they work in the garden they will experience how physical activity can be fun and productive.[32]

Adults can appreciate all the benefits that children get from helping in a garden but children may not right away. In order to help children develop an interest in gardening keep what they do simple, designate a specific area that they work on, involve them in the discussion about what should be grown, buy them their own tools, let them play in the dirt, plant flowers that will attract a variety of birds and insects and make your time outside with them fun. Some great activities to engage children in are watering, digging, planting, composting, harvesting, weeding and deadheading flowers. To help keep children safe in the garden avoid using harsh chemicals, keep sharp tools out of reach, make sure they are hydrated, apply sunscreen to exposed areas and supervise them while outside.[32]

Lessons Learned

I enjoy watching my food grow from seed and going from garden to table. Not only is it very satisfying to clear an area, plant seeds and maintain the produce through weeding and watering, what you get tastes far better than anything you buy in the grocery store. Gardening also proved to be very relaxing and calming, a time I always looked forward to.

Step back and consider...
...how many fresh fruits and vegetables you have on your kitchen counter.

Have you thought about.....

1. ...where you can have a garden whether you live in a house or an apartment?
2. ...what you could grow in a garden?
3. ...how different your life and that of your children would be if you spent time together in a garden?

21

Glass

Having considered the negative impacts of plastic, I overhauled my kitchen and replaced all my plastic storage containers with glass ones. Making the change to glass took some time but was a necessary next step on my journey towards improved health and a balanced life.

Plastic containers are cheaper, lighter to carry around and less breakable but the benefits of glass outweigh those of plastic. Purchasing glass containers is initially an expensive investment but over time you will save money due to the durability and reusability of glass. After years of use, glass will still maintain its shape and structural integrity. Unlike plastic, glass containers do not absorb the odor or color of the items stored in them, helping them to last longer. Since glass does not absorb any odors the taste of foods stored in it is not changed during the reheating process, as can happen with plastic. When food stored in glass is reheated, there are no concerns about toxic chemicals from the container being absorbed into the food. Drinking liquids in a reusable glass bottle, instead of a plastic one, reduces the toxic chemicals ingested that are leached out of the plastic. To minimize breakage using a glass water bottle buy glass bottles that are protected in a silicon sleeve. Since glass is not a porous surface, it does not absorb any of the bacteria it comes in contact with and can be cleaned at a high temperature.[33] Using glass storage allows you to easily organize your refrigerator and keep it clean since the contents are visible. Glass containers can conveniently go from the refrigerator to the oven to the table. Due to the reusable properties of glass there is less waste and less impact on the environment. When glass containers are recycled no harmful toxins are produced and emitted into the environment.[34] For all the reasons above, dry goods and other pantry items such as teas, flour and pasta should also be stored in glass.

Lessons Learned

Though plastic is ubiquitous and cheap it is not worth it when it comes to me and my family's health. Better to invest in a good set of glass containers than live a convenient, unhealthy life.

Step back and consider...
...what the items in your kitchen are stored in.

Have you thought about.....

1. ...how much glass you use daily?
2. ...the danger you are exposed to with constant use of plastic?
3. ...what you will do to significantly increase your use of glass?

22

Personal Care and Cleaning Items

As I was working on cleaning up my nutrition and my storage containers, my attention turned to my personal care items and cleaning supplies. I had always purchased manufactured personal care items and not thought much about it. As the rest of my life was getting cleaned out I did some research on the ingredient list for the items I used and was surprised to read about how dangerous some of the ingredients are. The smell of the cleaning supplies I used always bothered me and made cleaning a real challenge. I researched the ingredients of the cleaning supplies and found out how damaging and disruptive they can be.

Though they are convenient and promise great results, store bought, conventional personal care and cleaning supplies are made with a series of chemicals and compounds that can be very damaging to your health. There are at least 16 chemicals that can be found in common personal care and cleaning items that should be avoided:

1) Diethanolamine (DEA)
2) Monoethanolamine (MEA)
3) Triethanolamine (TEA)
4) Phthalates and Parabens
5) FD&C dyes
6) Fragrance
7) Imidazolidinyl Urea and DMDM Hydantoin,
8) Quaternium-15
9) Isopropyl Alcohol
10) Mineral Oil
11) Polyethylene Glycol (PEG)
12) Propylene Glycol
13) Sodium Lauryl Sulfate and Sodium Laureth Sulfate
14) Triclosan
15) Talc
16) Petroleum

Each of the ingredients found in cleaning and personal care items have several health risks associated. DEA, MEA, and TEA commonly found in shampoo, soap, bubble baths and facial cleansers can disrupt hormones and create cancer causing agents. Phthalates and Parabens used as preservative in cosmetics, such as hairspray and nail polish, are linked to causing cancer, particularly breast cancer. FD&C dyes are cancer causing and can cause skin sensitivity and irritation. Fragrances often found in shampoos, deodorants, sunscreens, skincare and body products are synthetic and can cause cancer. Imidazolidinyl Urea and DMDM Hydantoin, components of formaldehyde, are used in several personal care items and linked to allergies, depression, dizziness, ear infections, headaches, joint pain, loss of sleep, chest pain, chronic fatigue and can trigger asthma. Quaternium-15 used in many skin and hair products is known to cause allergic reactions and skin inflammation. Isopropyl Alcohol used in hair color rinses, body rubs, hand lotion and aftershave lotions destroy intestinal flora and can cause headaches, dizziness, depression, nausea, vomiting, and in some cases coma. Mineral oil prevents the skin from breathing, absorbing and excreting causing it to age prematurely. PEG, a degreaser, used in oven cleaners and skin and hair products strips the skin and body of protective oils leaving them more vulnerable to toxins. Propylene Glycol, the active ingredient in antifreeze, is used in makeup, toothpaste and deodorant and can lead to abnormalities in the brain, liver and kidneys.

When Sodium Lauryl Sulfate and Sodium Laureth Sulfate, very toxic ingredients found in makeup, shampoo, conditioner and toothpaste, are used with other chemicals they form nitrosamines, a very deadly carcinogen. Exposure to nitrosamines can cause eye damage, depression and other conditions. Triclosan an antibacterial ingredient used in soaps, disinfectant gels and toothpaste is highly toxic and disrupts hormones, can affect sexual function and fertility, lead to birth defects, suppression of the immune system, brain hemorrhages and heart problems. Talc, found in makeup, kids and adult powders and foundation, has been linked to ovarian and testicular cancer. Petroleum prevents the skin from breathing and excreting.[35]

As concerns for health become more prevalent and people become more aware of the dangerous effects cleaning chemicals and personal care products are having, they are going back to basics and looking for greener ways to take care of themselves. There are many benefits you will experience if you choose to make your own or buy personal care and cleaning products that are made with natural ingredients. You will enjoy a healthier home that is free of chemicals and toxins that can lead to a host of very serious problems. The air you breathe will be much purer and you will reduce the pollutants you are exposed to. There will be less chance of skin and eye irritation from using the harsh chemicals. The natural essential oils, such as tea tree, lavender, peppermint and lemon, used to make your household products will have a pleasant odor during cleaning. A lot of the ingredients used to make your own products are a lot cheaper to purchase or you may already have them on hand, therefore saving you money in the process. Homemade products will be free of antibacterial agents that can affect your hormonal and thyroid system. Knowing the above, you will be fully aware of the ingredients that you use for your personal care and cleaning products, which lead to a better quality of life for you and your family.[36]

Lessons Learned

It is worth the effort it takes to make my own personal care and household cleaning items. In order to reduce the toxic burden on my body and that of my family, it is necessary to make my own items. Making everything from toothpaste to body lotion and toilet bowl cleaner requires simple ingredients and will ensure a healthier, happier life.

Step back and consider...
...the ingredient list on your personal care and household cleaning items.

Have you thought about.....

1. ...the health issues that can be caused by your conventional personal care and cleaning products?
2. ...how the quality of your life will improve if you made your own products?
3. ...what products you are willing to make at home in order to reduce the health impacts of conventional products?

23

Business

Given all that I learned about the dangers of the ingredients in my conventional personal care and cleaning products, I started making my own. As I talked about all the different products I made for myself and the natural ingredients that I was using, people said they would be willing to buy the products from me. Realizing that there might be a market to purchase clean, natural products I considered the idea of starting a business. The idea of starting a business and selling something that had a demand was very appealing but I knew nothing about becoming an entrepreneur. As with other goals I had, I started to read everything I could about organizing and managing a business.

The first thing I read about was what characteristics are necessary to become a successful business owner. It was important for me to know the type of person I needed to be if I was to succeed. There are several traits that a small business owner needs to have. The first necessary trait is to be driven to succeed. The individual must be driven enough to push through the different challenges they will face as they start and develop the business. The individual must also be goal oriented and be able to focus on the action steps necessary to reach the goal. A certain amount of confidence is necessary to develop trust, respect and success. The person must be passionate about the work they are involved in. The business owner must be very organized and disciplined when it comes to managing their budget. Some businesses may require a team to be successful but the business owner must still be able to think and act independently. Even though the entrepreneur must be able to act independently they must also be humble and open to input and criticism.

Given the challenges a small business owner faces, the individual needs to be resilient and able to refocus after a setback.[37] Due to the unpredictable nature of being a business owner the individual needs to be flexible, able to handle uncertainty and the fear of failure. Self-confidence, the certainty that you are selling what others want, is critical for an entrepreneur. The business owner must be willing to accept a certain amount of risk as they move their READER REʸard.[38]

Once I understood some of the different traits that are necessary to start a business and considered my own character I decided to move ahead. Having the right character and mindset is only part of the equation; I also needed to understand the legal expectations and requirements. Businesses can take different forms: they can be a limited liability company (LLC), a sole proprietor operation, or a corporation. After considering each business form I chose to become an LLC. An LLC is a separate and distinct legal entity that has its own tax ID number and bank account. The main advantage of being an LLC is that the owner is not personally responsible for the financial obligation and debt of the LLC. The owner of an LLC pays taxes on the profits of the business at their own individual tax rate, this is different than the other forms of business. [39] The next required step was to get my business license from the state and an occupational license from my town. Each state and town is different so I had to search out the information specific to my area. Sales tax requirements also vary so research was necessary to determine my obligations. As a home business owner living in a rental property it was necessary for me to find out if there were any restrictions in place. The property owner was required to approve the use of some space for the business.

After fulfilling all the legal requirements the next thing to understand was the process of running the business. The first thing to realize was that I would get out of it what I put in to it. In large part, the success I experience will depend on what I am willing to invest in the business. In order to put in what is necessary I must enjoy what I do and look forward to putting in the time. Not only must I enjoy what I do, I must believe in the products themselves and the future success of the business. To be successful a plan must be in place that will help to develop, implement and maintain the business going forward. The space that will be used for the business should be well organized and thought out. Systems and routines for business activities should be in place to help accomplish as much as possible. Managing the money received from product sales and the money spent on inventory and supplies must be tracked closely to ensure accurate accounting. Quality ingredients and packaging must be sourced from reputable and reliable providers. The price point for the products should ensure a profit. If no profit is generated from a business it is considered a very expensive hobby. Once the business foundation has been laid, the process of selling must begin. A business owner has to be actively talking about their business and selling their products. Taking the time to carefully lay the foundation of your business will not matter if no one is asked to purchase what you make. It is important to understand your target customer and know how to best reach them. There are multiple ways to gain visibility but pursue only those that will reach your target customer considering who they are. Part of gaining visibility is understanding how best to utilize the internet and social media. Understanding how to set up your website and which platforms to use is important for the success of your business. There are many E-commerce sites available but research is necessary to determine which one will be best for you and your business. A business owner must understand what sets them apart from other businesses selling a similar product. To stay competitive it is important to take time to read different publications, visit websites, join business associations and network with other business owners.

With all that is necessary to manage a successful business, the owner still needs to be easily accessible to customers. Take time to support different initiatives and charities that are designed to improve the local community where you do business. Though it is time consuming to manage a successful business it is still important to build in time for breaks, self-care and relaxation.[40]

Lessons Learned

There is a lot to navigate and understand about being a business owner and this endeavor should not be entered into lightly. It is essential to know the legal requirements, the type of character traits necessary, and how to successfully manage a business. Though there can be many challenges to owning a business and success is not immediate it is still worth pursuing, knowing I am going after my dream.

> *Step back and consider...*
> ...if you have the character to be your own boss.

Have you thought about.....

1. ...what it would be like to go into business for yourself?
2. ...what type of products that are in demand could you sell?
3. ...how others would be impacted by your business?

24

Meditation

As I pursued the different goals of motherhood, triathlon, starting a personal care business and becoming a coach, I found myself in a state of constant thought. My mind was always racing and thinking of what I was going to do next. This consuming activity left me feeling overwhelmed and unable to relax. I needed some mental peace and decided to try meditation after having heard of its many benefits while listening to an interview on an online health summit.

Some of the psychological benefits experienced from meditation are: reduced stress, improved concentration and focus, the desire to have a healthier lifestyle, increased self-awareness, increased happiness, increased acceptance, improved creativity and relaxation.[41] The physical benefits of following a daily meditation practice are: lower blood pressure, a reduced number of anxiety attacks, a decrease in pain related tension, improved mood, improved immune system and an increased level of energy.[42]

Meditation can be anything that allows you to pause, to step outside of the busy pace of life and relax and refocus. For some that might be a walk in nature, listening to instrumental music, sitting by a body of water or joining others in a meditation class. The best way to experience the many benefits of meditation is to incorporate a few minutes of it into your daily routine. Taking just a few minutes each day can do wonders for your emotional, mental and physical state. When I thought of meditation I always envisioned someone sitting on the floor, legs crossed, open palms on knees chanting but that is not necessarily the case. Meditation can take many forms. For me the most effective method is to sit in a comfortable position for a predetermined amount of time. During my daily meditation practice I might listen to a guided meditation or focus on a mantra, chant, of my choosing. As you consider starting a meditation practice, it is important to find something that best suits you. Knowing the benefits that come from meditating, the temptation can be to start out thinking that the longer, the better but that will only leave you feeling frustrated. Plan to meditate for a couple of minutes initially. When you begin meditating, it is very hard to calm the mind because we are all so busy thinking that we cannot take time to pause and be still. Be patient with yourself, when you find yourself being distracted in thought acknowledge it and refocus. Over time you will find yourself able to focus more and more. As your level of focus improves, increase the amount of time you commit to your practice. There is no set length of time that you should meditate, even a few minutes can have an impact. Having said that, fifteen to twenty minutes will allow you to experience maximum benefit. Time becomes the limiting factor, a few minutes of meditation a day is better than none for your overall health and well-being.[43]

Lessons Learned

Meditation has become a regular part of my daily routine. I look to it daily as a way to take a pause and just be still in what is otherwise a very busy life. The timed meditation application I found provides background music as I take time to relax and clear my mind. Most days I meditate for ten minutes and some days it is two minutes, either way I come away feeling better for it.

Step back and consider...
        ...when you last took time out to pause.

Have you thought about.....

1. ...your current level of stress?
2. ...how different you will feel throughout the day if you take just a few minutes to pause and meditate?
3. ...when and what would be the best form of meditation for you?

25

Words

Both of my parents have been educators for many, many years, my father is a professor of agriculture and my mother is a teacher with her doctorate. They are both lifelong learners and worked to instill the love of learning in their children. My mother and father made sure that we understood the importance and meaning of words and were taught to use the dictionary at an early age. Our summers were full of reading books on a variety of topics. Words were an important part of our lives beyond our conversations as a family.

As I became an adult my command of the English language was very good and I became an avid reader. My parents instilled in me the love of books and words, something I did not fully appreciate as a child. As an adult, I enjoy learning about new things and have a large library that includes books from a wide variety of topics. Throughout the years I have collected books on running, triathlon, cooking, decluttering, God, crocheting, chess and biographies on the famous and not so famous. In my reading I came across a book that discussed the power of words to do more than impart knowledge. Being fascinated by the deeper impact of words I read a lot of articles and books to see what I could learn and apply.

I learned how words have the ability to change our physiology. Positive words like peace and love can change our gene expression, propel the motivational centers of our brain into action and build resiliency. Just as powerfully, negative words can negatively affect the production of genes that protect us from stress.[44] Dwelling on a positive word can lead to a positive view of yourself and others while dwelling on a negative word can lead to low self-esteem, anxiety and suspicion of others. Focusing on negative thoughts can further negatively affect your appetite, sleep and happiness. Over time the thoughts you dwell on will change the structure of your brain and its response to words therefore changing your perception of reality. Words that instill fear and anxiety like illness, death and poverty stimulate the brain in negative ways. Once the brain is stimulated, even though the fearful thoughts are not real and irrational, the brain will respond to them as though they are occurring in reality.[45]

A change in the word you use to define yourself or a situation can intensify or minimize the emotion associated with it. If you say "great" instead of "good" when someone asks how you are you will think and feel better. Saying "stretched" instead of "overwhelmed" during a tough time will lighten your perception of what you are experiencing.[46] The words you use in conversation, whether intended or not, can change the emotions of the individual with whom you are talking. People are impacted positively or negatively by words used in conversations. The listener can be left feeling more irritable, anxious and less trusting of others.

Repeated use of positive words can counter the effects of negative words. Due to the fact that our brains are hardwired to respond more rapidly to negative words that threaten our survival, we need to generate many more positive words. For every negative word we think of we need to consciously focus on three positive words to counter its effect. This also holds true in business and personal relationships where five positive comments are necessary to counter the effects of one negative comment or criticism. Even if the positive thoughts you have are irrational in the moment they will lead to a sense of happiness and wellbeing. The positive thoughts you have will leave you feeling more encouraged about your life.[44]

Lessons Learned

I must take what I think and say very seriously because words, whether spoken or thought, have the ability to make a big difference in my emotional state. I can make situations better or worse simply by using certain words. Words have an effect on my physiology and can negatively or positively impact my health. Conscious effort is needed to choose words that lead to a balanced life.

Step back and consider...
...the last thought or conversation you had.

Have you thought about.....

1. ...whether your words are primarily negative or positive?
2. ...how your words, whether spoken or thought, are impacting your life?
3. ...which positive words you will incorporate into your vocabulary to improve your emotional and physiological state?

26

Smile

Growing up my mother would often tell me and my siblings to smile. She said there is always a reason to smile. At the time I would muster a smile and then go on about my day. Sometimes when I heard her I would genuinely smile and at other times I would smile only because she said it but had no emotion behind it. What she asked me to do as a child helped me smile more often and generally have a more cheerful temperament as an adult.

The full impact and significance of her request to smile as a child came to me about a year ago when I was training to run my second half marathon after having my second daughter. Looking to improve my performance and get back to my pre-pregnancy race time, I made an effort to do my best. As I searched through books and articles during training I was reminded of a world famous triathlete, Chrissie Wellington, who smiles the entire way through her ironman races. Smiling through a race that includes: a 2.4 mile swim, 114 miles on the bike followed by a 26.2 mile run is no small feat. She attributes smiling for her success. With her in mind, I decided to smile my way through my half marathon race. During the race, I worked to have a smile on my face whether it was due to thinking of happy times or simply forcing it to be there. To my surprise, I did amazingly well and felt better than I had before in my previous races. After experiencing the power of a smile in my race, I decided to read more about its impact in more depth.

What I discovered about a smile was very interesting. Researchers at UC Berkeley conducted research on students in an old yearbook. They found those who smiled widest had more fulfilling and longer lasting marriages, had a better sense of well-being, were generally happier and were more inspiring to others. A smile is one of the most basic, biologically uniform expressions of all humans. Paul Ekman, the world's leading expert on facial expressions, discovered that smiles are cross-cultural and have the same meaning in different societies. Humans smile naturally and use it to positively impact just about every social situation. Children smile as many as 400 times per day! Surprisingly, over 30% of the adult population smiles more than 20 times a day and less than 14% smile less than 5 times a day. Smiling is contagious; when we see a smile we have an uncontrollable innate desire to smile, even if it is a smile from a stranger.[47] Our brains are able to distinguish between a real smile and a fake smile. Researcher Dr. Neidenthal proposes there are three ways we are able to do that. First our brains compare the geometry of a person's face to a standard smile. Second consider the situation and determine if a smile is warranted. The third method we use is we mimic the smile ourselves to feel whether it is genuine. If the smile we see is real we will stimulate the same areas of our brain and conclude whether it is real. Charles Darwin developed the Facial Feedback Response Theory, which suggests that the simple act of smiling actually changes our physiology and makes us feel better. Smiling stimulates our brain's reward center in a way that even chocolate cannot.[48]

British researchers found that one smile can provide the same level of brain stimulation as up to 2,000 chocolate bars. They also found that smiling can be as stimulating as receiving up to £16,000 ($19,449.40) in cash.[49] Smiling has many documented therapeutic effects, such as reduced stress hormone levels (like cortisol, adrenaline, and dopamine), increased health and mood boosting hormone levels (like endorphins), and lowered blood pressure.[47]

One of the greatest things about smiling is that it can be relearned from our childhood, a time when we smiled genuinely up to 400 times a day. There are four things you can do to relearn how to smile more. The first way is to think of a happy time in your life that brought great satisfaction and joy. The second way is to take time to smile at yourself in the mirror. Smiling at yourself will help you activate your mouth corners and your eye sockets generating a genuine smile. That genuine smile will result in feeling happy and relaxed. The third way is to simply become comfortable with smiling throughout your day no matter what is going on.[45] The fourth thing you can do is simply pause throughout the day and tell yourself to smile.

Lessons Learned

A smile is a simple act that can be easily ignored but has powerful effects over our body, our mind and others around us. The smile helped me with one race and has the power to help me in so many other situations I face throughout my life. I need to consciously smile more every day and especially when times are challenging.

Step back and consider...
   ...the beauty of your smile.

Have you thought about.....

1. ...how often you smile throughout the day?
2. ...how different your life could be if you smiled more?
3. ...what you will do to help yourself smile more?

Epilogue

I have learned a lot on my journey towards health and a balanced life. After living in a house in Connecticut for 17 years, my family moved to Minnesota where we lived in an apartment for a year. Moving to a new environment and living in a different situation, in an apartment and with a young baby, forced me to reevaluate how to implement what I had learned about health and balance. I knew that I was benefiting from the transformation I had undergone and needed to find a way to maintain it.

Moving into a new town poses many challenges but it was very important to find ways to connect as a family in our new environment as we each got settled. I made an effort to find the local co-op so that we could resume healthy eating and did not have to rely on fast food. We did not have a yard to plant a garden so we grew some herbs and vegetables on the porch. My baby was waking up frequently during the night so I took naps as necessary and was content with getting less sleep. I set goals for running races but was flexible about my training if I had to skip a day due to the needs of my family. When my baby napped I took time for self-care so I could greet her feeling refreshed when she woke up. I joined the local YMCA to establish a community of like-minded people with whom to interact. I took the lessons I learned from my coach about creating a balanced training schedule and implemented them as I coached myself through two half-marathons.

After a year in Minnesota we moved to a condo in Vermont. Once again I considered my new surroundings and implemented health and balance given what was available. No matter where life takes us we are always on a transformational journey towards health and balance.

Bibliography

Chapter 1

1. Duft, William. "Refined Sugar - The Sweetest poison of All...", www.quantumbalancing.com/news/sugar_blues.htm

Chapter 2

2. Batmanghelidj, F. MD. *Water: for Health, for Healing, for Life*, Warner Book, 2003
3. Mercola, Joseph Dr. "If You're Tired, You are Probably Lacking This", *Mercola.com*, www.articles.mercola.com/sites/articles/archive/2011/02/21/ how-drinking-spring-or-filtered-water-can-improve-your- health.aspx, February 21, 2011

Chapter 3

4. Pulde, Alona. MD and Matthew Lederman, M. "What is a Whole-Food, Plant-Based Diet?", *Forks Over Knives*, www.forksoverknives.com/what-to-eat/, May 15, 2014
5. Gunnars, Kris, BSc. "Leptin and Leptin Resistance: Everything You Need to Know", *Authority Nutrition*, www.authoritynutrition.com/leptin-101/
6. Mercola, Joseph Dr. "9 Ways That Eating Processed Food Made the World Sick and Fat", *Dr. Mercola.com*, www.articles.mercola.com/sites/articles/archive /2014/02/12/9- dangers-processed-foods.aspx, February 12,2014

Chapter 4

7. Walljasper, Jay. "Why Life in the Fast Lane Fails to Fulfill Us.", *Jay Walljasper*, www.jaywalljasper.com/articles/life-in-

the-fast-lane.html, published in the book LESS IS MORE (2009)

8. Rodriguez, Diana. "How to Lead a Well-Balanced Life", *Everyday Health*, www.everydayhealth.com/healthy-living/how-to-live-a-well-balanced-life.aspx, May 20, 2009

Chapter 5

9. Celes. "6 Important Reasons Why You Should Set Goals", *Personal Excellence*, www.personalexcellence.co/blog/why-set-goals/

Chapter 6

10. Wellness Mama. "The Dangers of Plastic", *Wellness mama.com*, www.wellnessmama.com/23757/dangers-of-plastic/, October 25, 2016

Chapter 7

11. "Take Care of Your Chronic Illnesses", www.ahealthiernc.com/gethealthy/whatdoes healthymean/language/en-us

Chapter 9

12. Mayo Clinic Staff, "Exercise: 7 Benefits of Regular Physical Activity", www.mayoclinic.org/healthy-lifestyle/fitness/in-depth/exercise/art-20048389, Oct. 13, 2016

Chapter 10

13. Monroe, Suzanne, "Nuggets of Wisdom with Various Diets", *Get Real Plan*, www.iawpclassroom.com /mod/book/tool

Chapter 11

14. Roberts, Emily MA, LPC, "Why Self-Care is Important for

Your Physical and Mental Health", *Healthy Place,*
www.healthyplace.com/blogs/buildingselfesteem/2015
/09/why-self-care-is-important-for-your-mental-physical-
health/, September 12, 2015

Chapter 12
15. Mercola, Joseph Dr. "The Many Reasons Why You Need
    Sleep", *Mercola.com,* www.articles.mercola.com/
    sites/articles/archive/2015/10/15/why-you-need-sleep.aspx,
    October 15, 2015
16. "Twelve Simple Tips To Improve Your Sleep", *Healthy
    Sleep,* www.healthysleep.med.harvard.ed, u/healthy/
    getting/overcoming/tips, December 18, 2007
17. "Healthy Sleep Tips", *National Sleep Foundation,*
    www.sleepfoundation.org/sleep-tools-tips/ healthy-
    sleep-tips

Chapter 13
18. Hereford, Z. "Self-Discipline – The Foundation
    for Success", *Essential Life Skills,* www.essentiallifeskills.
    net/ self-discipline.html
19. Sasson, Remez. "Self-Discipline Benefits and Importance",
    Success Consiousness, www.successconsciousness.com
    /self_discipline.htm

Chapter 14
20. "50 Reasons to Join a Running Club", *Savannah
    Strider Track Club,* www.savystrider.com/content.aspx?
    pageid=22&club_id=38931&module_id=131382

Chapter 15
21. "Cultivate the Healing Power of Gratitude", *The Chopra
    Center,* www.chopra.com/articles/cultivate-the-healing-
    power-of-gratitude

22. Fabrega, Marelisa. "How Gratitude Can Change Your Life", *The Change Blog*, www.thechangeblog.com /gratitude/

23. Borchard,Therese. "6 Ways to Cultivate Gratitude", *Everyday Health*, www.everydayhealth.com/ columns/therese-borchard-sanity-break/6-ways-to-cultivate-gratitude/, November 25, 2013

Chapter 16

24. Beattie, Darren. "How to Hire a Good Coach", *Skill Based Fitness*, www.skillbasedfitness.com/how-to-hire-a-good-coach/

25. Rakestraw, Ken. " 6 Benefits of Training with a Coach", *BSX Athletics*, www.blog.bsxtechnologies.com /2013/09/12/6-benefits-of-training-with-a-coach/, September 12, 2013

26. Lobby, Mackenzie. "The Benefits of Hiring a Triathlon Coach", *Active.com*, www.active.com/triathlon/articles/the-benefits-of-hiring-a-triathlon-coach

Chapter 18

27. "The Advantages of Family Time", *South University*, www.southuniversity.edu/whoweare/newsroom/blog/the-advantages-of-family-time-113366, November 20, 2012

Chapter 19

28. McAllister, Joseph. "Benefits of Eating Homemade Meals", *Livestrong.com*, www.livestrong.com/article/489114-benefit- of-eating-homemade-food/, Jun 10, 2015

29. Roizman, Tracey, D.C. "The Advantages of a Home Cooked Meal", www.SFGate healthyeating.com /advantages-home-cooked-meal-1930.html

Chapter 20

30. Darnton, Julia and Lauren McGuire. "What are the Physical and mental benefits of gardening?" Michigan State University Extension, www.msue.anr.msu.edu/news/what_are_the_physical_and_ mental_benefits_of_ gardening, May 19, 2014

31. Eliades, Angelo. "Wellbeing Gardening-Gardening for the Body, Mind and Spirit" *Permaculture Research Institute*, www.permaculturenews.org/2013/06/05/wellbeing-gardening-gardening-for-the-body-mind-spirit/, June 5, 2013

32. "Gardening for children" *Better Health Channel*, www. betterhealth.vic.gov.au/health/healthyliving/gardening-for-children, August 2014

Chapter 21

33. Gaga. "Why Glass Food Storage Containers are Better Than Plastic" *Healthy Cookware*, www.healthy-cookware.com/why-glass-food-storage-containers-are-better- than-plastic/, June 24, 2015

34. Thompson, Lorraine. "Are You Afraid of Your Plastic Food Containers? Replace Them With Glass" *Copywriter's Kitchen*, www.copywriterskitchen.com/2009/02/27/are-you-afraid-of-your-plastic-food-containers/, February 27, 2009

Chapter 22

35. Lipman, Frank. "14 Chemicals to Avoid in Your Personal Care Products" January 23, 2013

36. Weber, Carol Ruth. "7 Benefits of Green Cleaning" *Care.com*, www.care.com/c/stories/5919/7-benefits-of-green-cleaning/

Chapter 23

37. Gregory, Alyssa. "10 Character Traits of Successful Small Business Owners" *The Balance*, www.thebalance.com/ successful-owners-character-traits-2951855, September 29, 2016

38. Robinson, Joe. "The 7 Traits of Successful Entrepreneurs" *Entrepreneur*, www.entrepreneur.com/article/230350 January 10, 2014

39. "What is an LLC?" *Total Legal*, www.totallegal.com/ business/llc.aspx?src=gvtfr1&gclid=CM236oagr NACFY5MDQodQnAFRA

40. James Stephenson, James. "25 Common Characteristics of Successful Entrepreneurs" *Entrepreneur*, www.entrepreneur.com/article/200730

Chapter 24

41. Crane, Kristine. "8 Ways Meditation Can Improve Your Life" *Us News*, www.health.usnews.com/health-news /health- wellness/slideshows/8-ways-meditation-can-improve-your-life, September 12, 2014

42. "Benefits of Meditation" *The Art of Living*, www.artofliving.org/us-en/meditation/meditation- for-you/benefits-of-meditation

43. Bodhipaksa. "How long should I meditate each day?" *Wildmind Buddhist Meditation*, www.wildmind.org/ mindfulness/four/how-long-should-i-meditate-each-day, February 25, 2013

Chapter 25

44. Borchard, Therese J. "Words Can Change Your Brain" *Everyday Health*, www.everydayhealth.com/columns/ therese-borchard-sanity-break/420/, August 13, 2013

45. Newberg, Andrew M.D. and Mark Waldman. "Words Can

Change Your Brain" *Psychology Today*, www.psychology
today.com/ blog/words-can-change-your-brain/201208/
the-most-dangerous-word-in-the-world, August 1, 2012

46. Robbins, Anthony. *Awaken the Giant Within: How to Take
Immediate Control of Your Mental, Emotional, Physical
and Financial Destiny*, Free Press, 2003

Chapter 26

47. Gutman, Ron. "The Untapped Power of Smiling" *Forbes*,
www.forbes.com/sites/ericsavitz/2011/03/22/the-untapped-
power-of-smiling/#66b3a1ae20d8, March 22, 2011

48. Smile Direct Club, "The Power of a Smile"
www.smiledirectclub.tumblr.com/post/124156747639/the-
power-of-a-smile-7-facts-about-smiles, Jul 15, 2015

49. Widrich, Leo. "The Science of Smiling: A Guide to the
World's Most Powerful Gesture" *Life Hacking*,
www.blog.bufferapp.com/the-science-of-smiling-a-guide-
to-humans-most-powerful-gesture, April 1, 2016

Deeper Dive

List of recommended books to explore the topics in more depth.

Virgin, JJ. *Sugar Impact Diet: Drop 7 Hidden Sugars, Lose Up to 10 Pounds in Just 2 Weeks.* Grand Central Life & Style, 2014

Burchard, Brendon. *The Motivation Manifesto: 9 Declarations of Claim Your Personal Power.* Hay House Inc., 2014

Terry, Beth. *Plastic Free: How I Kicked the Plastic Habit and How You Can Too.* Skyhorse Publishing, 2012

Bingham, John. *The Courage to Start: A Guide to Running for Your Life.* Fireside, 1999

Carmichael, Chris and Jim Rutberg, *The Time-Crunched Triathlete: Race-Winning Fitness in 8 Hours a Week.* Velo Press, 2010

Hyman, Mark MD. *Eat Fat, Get Thin: Why the Fat We Eat is the Key to Sustained Weight Loss and Vibrant Health.* Little, Brown and Company, 2016

Duhigg, Charles. *The Power of Habit: Why We Do What We Do in Life and Business.* Random House Trade Paperback, 2014

Seymour, John. *The New Self-Sufficient Gardener* Dorling Kindersley Ltd, 2008

Paulson, Ed. *The Complete Idiot's Guide to Starting Your Own Business*. Alpha Books, 2012

Robbins, Anthony. *Awaken the Giant Within: How to Take Immediate Control of Your Mental, Emotional, Physical and Financial Destiny*. Free Press, 2003

Schwartz, David J. Ph.D., *The Magic of Thinking Big*. Fireside, 2007

Made in the USA
Middletown, DE
06 May 2017